HOW EMOTIONALLY MATURE ARE YOU?

The School of Life

Published in 2024 by The School of Life
930 High Road, London, N12 9RT
First published in the USA in 2025

Copyright © The School of Life 2025

Designed and typeset by Ryan Bartaby
Printed in China by Leo Paper Group

All rights reserved. This book is sold subject to the condition that it shall not be resold, lent, hired out or otherwise circulated without prior consent of the publisher.

A proportion of this book has appeared online at:
theschooloflife.com/articles

Every effort has been made to contact the copyright holders of the materials reproduced in this book. If any have been inadvertently overlooked, the publisher will be pleased to make restitution at the earliest opportunity.

The School of Life publishes a range of books on essential topics in psychological and emotional life, including relationships, parenting, friendship, careers and fulfilment. The aim is always to help us to understand ourselves better – and thereby to grow calmer, less confused and more purposeful. Discover our full range of titles, including books for children, here: www.theschooloflife.com/books

The School of Life also offers a comprehensive therapy service, which complements, and draws upon, our published works:
www.theschooloflife.com/therapy

www.theschooloflife.com

ISBN 978-1-915087-12-6

10 9 8 7 6 5 4 3 2 1

HOW EMOTIONALLY MATURE ARE YOU?

A guide to psychological adulthood

CONTENTS

I.	INTRODUCTION	6
II.	THE QUESTIONNAIRE	12
III.	SCORES & CONCLUSIONS	144

INTRODUCTION

Given the importance of emotional maturity to the state of our marriages, careers, childhoods and nations, it is striking how little direct attention is given to the subject. Of all the goals humans set themselves, emotional maturity might attract the least official recognition. We celebrate people's birthdays, not the day they stopped projecting their fears or shed their defensiveness. We award people prizes for throwing a javelin or floating companies on the stock exchange, never for their skill at saying sorry. We behave as though emotional maturity were a haphazard trinket of the soul, rather than – as it is – the central achievement of which any human is capable.

One of the reasons why growing up emotionally is seldom feted is that the process leaves no visible trace. We make a big deal of physical maturation, in part because we can so easily see it – we're under no illusion as to who might be the more senior when we compare an adolescent and a toddler, a midlifer and a pensioner. But when it comes to emotional maturity, it becomes far harder to determine what specimen we might have on our hands – and hence how many candles we might have to put on their metaphorical cake. A 52-year-old might, in terms of their underlying emotional development, be arrested at the age of 8. A 12-year-old might display the poise and empathy more associated with someone in their 40s.

What we mean by emotional maturity is a person's progress towards a range of psychological qualities: wisdom, poise, competence, self-knowledge, perspective, self-love, confidence and kindness. A priority for those seeking to become more mature should therefore be to take a measure of their development in order to be clearer about where work remains to be done.

The intention behind this questionnaire is that we might, thanks to a series of carefully structured enquiries, learn more about our specific immaturities and so put into place certain lessons and ideas that have the power to help us progress. By doing this, we might – with luck – spare ourselves a few decades of mistakes, and many crises, too.

The essays that accompany the questions are conduits to self-reflection and prompts for emotional exploration; we might spend as much time on reflection as we do on reading. We are invited to recognise ourselves in certain doubtful or counterproductive pen portraits – and sometimes to wince and perhaps vow to do things differently.

It may be best to answer the questions fast. 'Not thinking too much' can help our true natures to manifest themselves more cleanly. Speed can help us to catch our defences unaware. The inside back flap of the book has space to record our answers. Once we have worked through the series, we can retrace our steps and (using the grading system on page 147) add up our scores, which are designed to give us a sense of our overall level of maturity.

As ever, we should not expect to be entirely mature in all areas: imperfection is the general rule; we are never done with 'growing up'. We should be patient: being an adult is a supreme achievement – and one we seldom receive systematic instruction in, or reminders about. This book introduces us to some of our less developed dimensions and their correctives – in the name of the mature self we long for.

THE QUESTIONNAIRE

1. Someone politely suggests that you should probably 'grow up' a bit. How might you respond?

---

a) Take offence: you are well past the age of maturity.

---

b) Sigh. Agree.

The process of emotional maturity is humbling, as it refuses to follow the expected rules of ageing. We can be reasonably sure that over the years we will acquire more experience, more memories and, with a fair wind, somewhat more status and money. But when it comes to emotional maturity, humblingly and maddeningly, having been on the Earth for a certain amount of time guarantees us nothing at all.

There are 65-year-olds who, measured in terms of their emotional development, have stayed at the level of a toddler. There are 10-year-olds who show a grace and maturity more commonly to be expected in people in their 40s. In a smart restaurant frequented by the cities elite, a leading investment banker may speak to their partner in the tone of an aggrieved infant; in the suites of smart hotels, there may be howls of rage that more justly belong in nurseries. There are cardiac surgeons, treasury officials and high court judges who – in relation to their levels of poise and empathy – deserve to be dressed in short trousers. If there were schools devoted to emotional education, people in their 40s would be placed in certain classrooms alongside 6-year-olds.

A tempting response to this perplexing situation is to deny that it could exist; to cling to our physical age and worldly position as evidence of being a proper grown-up. But a wiser path might simply be to accept that, in many areas, we clearly do owe far more to our early childhood than our faces or business cards might suggest. In the way we answer to an insult, respond to being ignored by our partner or react to someone's need for reciprocal affection, we may well be three or four decades behind our chronological age.

We have no option but to take these facts on the chin. We start to grow up a little when we can finally bear to acknowledge that we have, in certain ways at least, probably failed to become an adult.

2. **In which areas would you like to become more of an emotional adult?**

---

a) Stop this!

---

b) Let me start to draw up a list.

The most alarmingly childish characters are those who insist – with particular vehemence – that they cannot possibly be such a thing. Correspondingly, we grow in sanity and maturity precisely to the extent that we can stand to fathom our more irrational and immature dimensions.

A true emotional adult doesn't mind being probed as to the ways in which they still have yet to grow up; they will have a good – albeit broad – sense of where homework needs to be done. Perhaps they can never receive criticism without taking offence, or they cannot resist playing games with people who like them, or they still wait for signs of approval from a parent who died two decades ago. It may be hard for them to stop acting out these unhelpful patterns that more fairly belong to people who aren't yet the size of a chair. But at least they are aware of their frailties and, in their calm moments, are committed to finding remedies. These introspective types will not resist the hard work of acknowledgement. They won't be offended by their own emotional idiocy – for they can trust that it belongs to our species as a whole rather than emanating from a personal curse that must be evaded.

Those who should worry us are the confident, blithe ones who pretend not to understand what we are talking about when we describe how likely it is that someone may still be a child inside.

On an early dinner date, two lovers sizing each other up might be advised to ask each other a distinctly odd-sounding question: 'In what ways are you still a big baby?' The ones to watch out for aren't those who have a long list to present (from how they respond to anxiety and their way of dealing with their mother to their handling of their envy of an old schoolmate), but rather those who tilt back their heads, laugh broadly and say with puzzlement: 'What on earth are you talking about!?'

3. 'People spend too long navel-gazing these days.' What do you feel about this statement?

a) Broadly agree.

b) Broadly disagree.

There are, no doubt, some people on Earth who spend far too long looking inside themselves, who are overly committed to the project of self-knowledge and who care too intensely about introspection. But in reality, there are very few of them indeed.

Far more common is the *idea* of them, which is used by a certain constituency to caricature the whole project of psychological progression and understanding. These people will, for their own purposes, set up a false dichotomy: either one can be mired in tedious self-obsession and neurotic inner exploration, or one can put away the 'psychobabble' and get on with a sane, active and outward-looking life. This division has a surface plausibility to it because there clearly are a few ways of being concerned with one's own mind that don't lead anywhere fruitful. As with any activity, there are unhealthy ways of introspecting. But it would be as unfair to condemn the entire project of emotional maturation on the evidence of the occasional preening and self-important journaler as it would be to condemn the ambitions of literature on the basis of a few egregious airport novels.

On balance, the greater risks seem to lie at the unexamined end of the spectrum. There are far more of us who act entirely without insight into our motives, who have never bothered to reflect on our pasts and who don't notice the influence of our moods on our judgement.

Knowing ourselves remains a supreme challenge that is accompanied by immense fear and anxiety; there is so much inside us that it would be nicer to avoid. It would be deeply convenient if we could just 'get on with life', but our psyches have a habit – when neglected – of coming back to haunt us. They ensure that we will twitch, be unable to sleep, succumb to anxiety or have a breakdown until they are attended to. We shouldn't compound our difficulties by implying that there is any real alternative to gazing rather hard, and at some considerable length, into our deep selves.

4. You hear about an adult who, after a hard day at work, wept like a child in bed and then called their mother for comfort. How do you respond?

---

a) I feel a bit sick.

---

b) Good for them; they know what they need.

We make inordinate efforts to try to be grown up. Small children give us a measure of the pride we generally take in no longer being small when they rush to tell us that they are now 4 'and three quarters' or 8 'and two thirds'. We can't wait to be done with education, to be able to leave home, earn our own money and have a right to call ourselves adults.

It's therefore puzzling to have to acknowledge, despite all the graduations, promotions and pension schemes that we have mastered, that real adulthood is a more ambiguous state than we might once have supposed. The border between adult and child that we took to be impregnable and definitive is, from close up, far from such a thing.

When we were at school, our teachers may have looked like immensely accomplished beings, wholly cut off from the fear, silliness and self-doubt that we knew so well in our own hearts. But once we have reached their age, we're likely to realise that, in key ways, we are still the people we were back when we were very small. We will have carried a host of the uncertainties and needs of early childhood into the adult realm. We may be 44 and a senior executive in a company and yet still, in difficult moments, long to be comforted like a weepy child and told that it will all be OK.

It appears that we never fully outgrow the dependence and fragility of our young selves. It's a mark of maturity not to rebel against this humiliating realisation. We should wryly concede that we have no option but to lapse regularly into immature states. There is no need to condemn or punish such tendencies; they are as squarely part of us as bravery and self-discipline.

The emotionally mature adult may only seldom actually behave like a needy baby – but they always remain in touch with the bits of themselves that would love to.

5. A friend is looking glum and concerned. How would you be most likely to respond?

---

a) Point out the positives – and perhaps suggest that they cheer up.

---

b) Sit with the causes – and commiserate.

On the face of it, it seems unproblematic to be a cheerful person. What could possibly be wrong with trying to look on the bright side of things, always with a joke at the ready? What could be remotely sinister about being exuberant and working to resist glumness and sorrow?

The difficulty lies not so much in delighting in the positives, it arises when there is a related intolerance towards anything that might be dark or troubling. There is a particular kind of person who cannot sit with, or reconcile themselves to, sadness. They feel an internal obligation to jolly everyone and everything along. They don't merely love happiness; they are constitutionally opposed to anything that might be sombre, however real and necessary a confrontation with it might be.

It is as though, somewhere in their early years, they faced a sadness potentially so engulfing that they fled from it into the embrace of a robust jolliness that brooks no argument or exception. When we are sad, they point out that spring is on the way. When we want to give up, they remind us that there is a lot to be proud and hopeful about. When we are tempted to weep, they might sing or whistle a merry tune.

True emotional maturity depends on making our peace with a range of extremely unpleasant facts about our own natures, other people and the parameters of earthly existence: that we will never be as talented as we want, that we were perhaps badly let down in early life, that we will have to die with most of our dreams unfulfilled ... And yet, a real adult manages to find an equilibrium between despair on the one hand and denial on the other. They are able to balance their awareness of all that is rotten, cruel and sterile with an ongoing appreciation of what is still tender and possible. Their smiles differ from those of the jollying person: these smiles are at once warm and speckled with notes of realism and melancholy. The emotionally mature make no attempt to coerce anyone into positivity. We are allowed to be downcast in their presence; our own sadness doesn't threaten their integrity. They can take our tears without fear.

For the jollying person, however, misery of any kind is at risk of unleashing a terrifying encounter with undigested feelings of loss, hurt and grief. They are forced to ask everyone else around them to smile in a frantic attempt to ward off their unexplored traumas. It may seem like they don't care about our problems; it's more that they have neglected their own for far too long to have any energy, sympathy or creativity left over for us.

Whatever the charms of smiling people, what we really need are characters with enough knowledge of their sadness not to panic when we are in urgent need of a cathartic cry.

6. How often do you find yourself losing your temper – perhaps rather more than is deserved – with a malfunctioning toaster, a missing set of car keys, a delayed plane or with your child or partner?

---

a) WHERE ARE THE DAMN KEYS!?

---

b) Not so often.

There is a kind of response to frustration that we can instantly tell is excessive, misdirected and out of kilter. A drawer doesn't open and its user starts to growl and swear with vehemence. The printer jams (again) and its owner bangs their fist on the table and lets out a run of expletives. One of the children has left a plate in slightly the wrong place and a parent leaps up from the table and delivers a tirade on the selfishness and lack of manners of the young. We would, if we were in a generous mood, describe such people as 'irritable', but could serve up more vigorous alternative terms if these were called for.

In trying to understand and then overcome such irritability, a key step is to distinguish it from anger. The two emotions can seem very similar indeed – both tend to involve impolite words and raised voices – but they are crucially different. The angry person has a correct grasp of what has actually offended or outraged them; they know the true source of their complaint and have the focus and inner strength to address this promptly and directly.

The irritable person also happens to be deeply frustrated, but they have lost sight of the genuine cause of their upset because it is frightening or surrounded by taboos. Perhaps they were angry with their boss, but they now get in a temper with their 5-year-old child. They might be disappointed with themselves for their lack of sexual success, but they now behave grumpily around their siblings. They are humiliated by their low status, but they kick the printer.

Oddly, perhaps, the person whom we call irritable is likely to have been – and still to be – far too meek and too inclined to say nothing to those who irk them. However, this isn't the kind of good manners that we should respect and encourage because there is fury involved that has been swallowed and suppressed instead of dealt with – and so is prone to surge up at random on more innocent and tangential targets. The little boy who grew up enduring a bullying father with apparent calm turns into a man who slams his fist regularly into walls and screams when there is a hold-up at the check-in desk.

The origin of irritability tends to be poignant; its effects are far less so. It is an achievement of maturity when we can finally manage to get cross with the right people and things; when we are brave enough to identify our real enemies and have the battles we need to have when we need to have them – while we treat everyone else with the kindness and patience they keenly deserve.

7. Your boss calls you into their office and thanks you for a recent report you wrote, but they comment gently that the final paragraph was perhaps a bit confused and might benefit from a second go when time allows. What do you say to yourself?

---

a) That thing took ages – there's nothing wrong with the last paragraph.

---

b) Oh well! Fair enough; I'll take a look this evening.

There is a form of psychological sickness that particularly afflicts those who are highly precise, methodical and keen to do their best. These characters aren't merely perfectionists, they are acutely alarmed at having any of their imperfections identified by third parties. They live in dread of criticism, they are horrified by 'feedback', they balk at having things pointed out to them. They are, as psychology puts it, highly defensive.

For the defensive person, feedback is never just a casual call to improve this or that aspect of their behaviour; it isn't merely a well-intentioned observation about their prose style, attitude to punctuality or cooking skills. To them, feedback is a fundamental assault on their right to exist – which is why it creates such upset and has to be rebuffed with vehemence. The defensive person doesn't just hear that 'the final paragraph was perhaps a bit confused' – they hear that 'it would be better if you had never been born'. No wonder if they prefer not to listen.

The origins of the defensive personality lie in early childhood, with an experience of criticism or neglect so excessive and unmasterable that the slightest critique has a power to unbalance the adult self. The child who was routinely made to feel that they were unwanted and unlovable is at risk of growing into an adult for whom any criticism, however minor, will summon up vicious feelings of worthlessness and untenable fears of abandonment.

The irony is that it isn't only hard to tell the defensive person that their grammar might need improving or that their shoes aren't right for an occasion – it is even harder to get them to contemplate that they might be defensive in the first place. What greater insult! How outrageous! And yet if the idea can take hold in their mind in a suitably warm and thoughtful context, then it might gradually become easier for them to unwind their panic and anger over individual instances of criticism. They might feel sorry for themselves for the way their psyche has grown to interpret feedback, as opposed to angry with well-intentioned others for directing them to areas where improvement may be possible.

Criticism is never entirely pleasant. We should strive to grow into people whose relationship to their past means that it doesn't have to feel devastating.

8. How would you be most likely to complete the following sentence: 'When a lover makes a promise in a relationship, what's likely to happen is …'

a) '… that it will be broken.'

b) '… impossible to know. One can't say. It just depends.'

A peculiar feature of our minds is that they are often – without us quite realising – laden with strong impressions of what is going to happen. They believe that they know what men 'really' want or what women are 'truly' inclined to do; they have ideas about what compliments 'actually' mean and what setbacks are 'genuinely' a sign of.

As soon as life places us in particular settings, our minds leap into action and fill in the rest of the story. We don't need to study the specifics. We just know the future: that we are going to be rejected. That someone is mocking us. That we will be used. Except, of course, that none of this may in any way be true. These ideas may just be coming from inside our own imaginations; they may – as psychologists put it – merely be our 'projections'.

We project because our minds – sometimes for good reasons – generalise outwards from experience when trying to surmise the future. We make hypotheses about what will happen from what did happen. It sounds sensible – except when, especially in the emotional realm, we fall into the trap of unhelpful or plain misleading extrapolations from unrepresentative events.

Our father may have been cruel and unconcerned, but not every man is. Our mother did taunt us, but some women – and perhaps the one we've just met – can be very kind.

Unfortunately, our minds tend to be terrible at distinctions. Unaware of the mental models they are carrying, they may fail to determine the unique contours of the situations they are actually faced with. Instead, they quickly become cross or suspicious or distant from people who might be entirely undeserving of their coldness.

What should replace projection is a commitment to judging every new situation on its own merits. We should give up assuming that 'men' or 'women' are anything; we should wait to find out more from close examination of every example we encounter.

We accede to emotional maturity when we stop automatically judging the present through the biased eyes of our past, and let present reality be our primary, more judicious and frequently more hopeful guide to who and what is before us.

9. Unexpectedly, a taxi you ordered is late. It's a nuisance and a problem. How are you likely to act?

---

a) Lose your temper, panic and, eventually, shout.

---

b) Reformulate your plans, then gaze serenely out of the window; these things happen.

Rarely are the differences between people revealed so starkly as when it comes to episodes of stress. Some people seem able to endure such occurrences without suffering substantial injury or offence. They forget their umbrella and end up soaked – but no matter, it will make for an amusing story once they dry off in a couple of hours; their plane is delayed for half a day – what an opportunity to catch up on some messages and a new novel.

We might evaluate people according to how far they implicitly feel from 'the chaos': the primordial state of disorder, collapse, destruction and illogicality from which we emerged and to which we are, eventually, destined to return. For some, there is only the thinnest membrane between the present and this zone of entropic collapse. Very little is ever needed to evoke it. All it takes is for a pullover to shrink unexpectedly in the wash, and suddenly everything stable, coherent and good about their lives is at once called into question.

One of the most important functions that a parent is ever able to perform for their small child is that of soothing: the art of bearing someone across the valley of frustration and fear to a place of peace and safety, through the means of love (expressed in lullabies, stroked brows and kindly reassuring assessments).

Those who missed out on soothing are not hard to spot: they are the ones who scream the first moment that there is a financial hiccup, who can't imagine that they will survive a rumour and who lack any faith that it will be possible to buy an equally nice new pullover in due course. The psychoanalyst Donald Winnicott presciently observed about the excessively fearful that 'the catastrophe you fear *will* happen has *already* happened'. In other words, the origin of our present-day panics tends to lie in shocking events that we had to bear without soothing at an age when we lacked all necessary resources to master reality.

Once the height of a crisis has abated, the easily panicked should remember to mourn their pasts, not fear their futures.

10. A deeply irritating person once again causes you problems through their impossible behaviour. How might you respond?

---

a) Itemise their failings and curse them.

---

b) Wonder about their childhood.

One of the more unexpected moves that the emotionally mature know how to make in relation to the follies and frustrations of a life spent among other humans is to think a lot about people's childhoods.

This isn't, normally, what annoying situations invite us to do. The gruff, bearded colleague who fails to credit us for our work and boasts about their salary doesn't directly entice us to reflect on what they might have been like at the age of 5. The entitled guest in the restaurant who screams that they want a better table isn't exactly charming us into reflecting on their early years.

Nevertheless, if we're to have any chance of remaining calm around the many outwardly unsavoury characters whom we are unable to avoid, then we would be advised to become deeply curious about their journeys from toddlerhood to the present. We should hunt for the tender little boy or girl within the hardened and grumpy colossus. The primary basis on which we can remain calm and kind around others is via tireless reflection on the likely routes down which our enemies must have travelled to become the difficult, contorted people they are today – and to strive always to convert our irritation into compassion. No one is born boastful or vain, devious or vengeful. These are the shapes into which human personality ends up being moulded by adversity and neglect. It's because no one listened that someone ends up pulling off theatrical attention-seeking antics, and it is because there was no opportunity to get angry that someone emerges as resentful and sly.

We are rarely able to know in great detail what unfolded in the pasts of those who madden us, but it is always open to us to try to imagine the story of how a baby, innocent and docile in their cot, could with time grow up into a gnarled and vexing adult.

There may be a certain grim satisfaction in fixating on precisely how dreadful many (most) people are; but true calm will only be possible when we learn to instead go in search of those damaged little boys and girls, with their dungarees and gap-toothed smiles, who suffered childhoods that continue to unbalance their lives.

11. You have just sat down to work on a difficult project that you have avoided for too long when, without warning, a pneumatic drill starts up outside. It's the start of two weeks of road works. What do you think?

---

a) You've got to be kidding. It's as if they're doing this to wind me up!

---

b) What an annoying coincidence that the water mains needs updating – and just now!

Annoying things happen almost constantly: trains pull out of platforms as we approach them; taps snap off their moorings; shopping bags leak; suppliers go bankrupt; colleagues resign; cars break down. It is all – undoubtedly – maddening. But the question is, how much does it all, beneath the surface, have to feel intentional?

For a certain kind of personality, it is very hard to hold on to the idea that many of our troubles might come down to something as innocent as chance. It simply seems implausible that awful things might repeatedly unfold, at terribly inopportune moments, without some kind of malevolent intent being involved. It can't be just an accident that their dinner order went missing, that their cinema seat was double-booked or that their phone battery died … Why did their dry cleaning – and no one else's – end up being stolen and their new shoes spring a leak? Why is there a strange smell just next to where they are seated on the plane? How come there is a small beetle in their salad? It's as though someone is trailing them, undermining them, laying traps for them – and laughing at them. It seems as if there is some kind of conspiracy to humiliate them. (Why else have they been walking around all day with a sticker on the back of their coat, and why does their zip jam exactly ten minutes before an important dinner?) No wonder they become very cross indeed.

The sad and touching truth is that there is – of course – almost never any conspiracy at play. But the fact that it strongly feels like there is one tells us a lot about the origins of paranoid hypersensitivity: it is the bitter fruit of self-hatred. When we heartily dislike ourselves, it is only natural to have the impression that the world is ridiculing us in turn. The hotel concierge knows exactly how awful we are – that's why they've given us the room with the malfunctioning air-conditioning unit; the waiter has deep experience of our revoltingness – that's why they chose to drop a piece of butter on our trousers; the phone company knows that we are an idiot (and that we think dreadful things) – that's why they've made sure our phone gives out on the second day of our trip.

We may not have been given the chance to see that our suspicious natures are a symptom of a self-hatred that owes its origins not to the prevalence of conspiracies but to childhood dynamics – and for this, we deserve ongoing sympathy. The world doesn't hate us; we have simply learnt to have contempt for ourselves, which returns to haunt us in the form of suspected plots.

No one is actually laughing at us; we weren't loved properly and now don't like ourselves very much. That's the true outrage for which we should reserve our anger and our self-compassion.

12. You've been invited to meet someone important in their office. Midway through, you realise you very much need to go to the bathroom. What do you do?

---

a) Hold it in. It's too embarrassing to ask.

---

b) Ask where the bathroom is.

One of the central achievements of emotional maturity and self-love can be located in a rather unexpected place: the capacity to ask where the bathroom is. This might seem like an absurd thing to worry about asking for: why not simply make a request the moment the need arises?

For many of us, things are not nearly so simple. Our bodily priorities are hemmed in by appalling degrees of embarrassment. We would far prefer to sit uncomfortably for three hours than reveal the source of our agony. The likely reason is that, deep down, we feel – far more than we perhaps consciously recognise – revolting. We feel that we are not like other people: the clean ones and the good ones, the smiling ones and the fortunate ones, the sunny ones and the pure ones – all those who can jump up and cheerily say 'I'm so sorry to interrupt, but could you direct me to …'

No such breezy candour is possible for us, who sit cross-legged with our insides contorting themselves in muffled pain, because we harbour a terrible secret. We don't only need a pee or a poo; we feel – in our essence – like something akin to urine or a turd, like something extremely unclean and unacceptable. All the time, we are trying to fight off the implications of this appalling secret; we're trying to make sure that other people don't realise and that no smells are (as it were) emanating from us. But we're always in danger of being spotted for the repulsive thing we're convinced we are.

This helps to explain why asking for the bathroom should be such a trial. It's because we're so embarrassed and ashamed of so much about ourselves already: our faces, our voices, our shoulders, our skin, our existence. Asking for something bodily – a drink of water, a lower temperature – just threatens to draw yet more troubling attention to our being.

How fortunate the rapid-bathroom-askers are by comparison. The reason they can ask with such innocence is that, decades ago, someone will have made them feel that everything about them was more or less fine: getting muddy, feeling sad, having a tantrum. They had no need to hide or pretend to be someone else. They were loved for who they were – and it shows every day of their adult lives.

It turns out that one of the central indicators of emotional health lies in a highly unexpected and trivial-sounding area. We will have cause to feel very proud of ourselves the day we can feel appropriately aware of, and sorry for, our younger self – and can ask to pop out to the bathroom for a few moments without shame.

13. You are promoted at work and realise that a junior is relying on you to tell them whether or not you want them to participate on a project. Every time they see you, they look a little nervous and even a touch beseeching; this is a big deal for them. How do you react?

---

a) Secretly, if you're honest, it's not unpleasant to feel how much someone else relies on you.

---

b) You do everything in your power to let them know, as quickly as possible, where they stand.

One of the odder realisations of adult life is that, without acceding to a throne or being placed in command of an army, simply by steadily doing what is generally expected of people in the business world, we can gradually end up having power over other human beings. It might not be immense power – not the power to decapitate, anoint or enslave. It might just be the power to allocate someone a desk or decide who works on what team, who gets promoted or who is offered a contract. Nevertheless, in its way, this is power still. In our own circumscribed domain, we are the ruler.

We all begin in positions of radical powerlessness. In our early years, someone else will always have called the shots. They will have told us what to wear, when to leave the house and how to behave around strangers. They will have decided what we ate, how much money we got and what state it was acceptable to leave our bedroom in.

Those who tend to be most thrilled to accede to adult power are likely to be those whose first experience of power was especially difficult; those whose caregivers brooked no argument, those who were allowed no leeway from the rules and who had to hear, far more often than was comfortable, the barked command: 'Because I say so!'

What more natural response, if this was our cowed and trammelled beginning, than to handle the sword of power with more than standard pleasure. What temptation to try to correct some of our earlier humiliations and to make good some of the disguised injuries of our younger selves by deliberately maintaining a sphynx-like appearance when surveying the attentive and eager-to-please faces of new recruits or by leaving some long and tense pauses when negotiating with someone on the phone.

It takes true maturity to resist using power to make others uncomfortable. We know that we are mature when we are no longer tempted to inflict on others a version of the pain that was inflicted on us; when we can allow others the terror-free growth that we were denied. The truly powerful have overcome their envy of those who may have had an easier life than they had; they have learnt to be more interested in kindness than domination.

14. You're not a particularly great or eager cook. You were looking forward to getting a takeaway supper for yourself from your favourite Indian restaurant when you suddenly learn that some important friends are going to be coming round. What do you do?

---

a) Scramble urgently to lay the table elegantly – and rustle up a formal three-course meal.

---

b) Plan to offer your friends a takeaway too.

Navigating adult life forces us to ask ourselves – implicitly – a rather peculiar-sounding question: what are other people like? By this we mean, among other things, what are they excited by? What makes them anxious? What do they enjoy? How do they relax?

Our answers end up heavily determining how we behave socially: what do we dare to chat about? How do we assess people's needs? And what should we prepare them for dinner?

We can hazard the generalisation that most of us start off with a very unrealistic picture of others, skewed in a direction of excessive formality and conventionality. When we are small children, our parents and teachers seem big, competent, endlessly knowledgeable and hugely serious. We don't impute to them most of the emotions that we know from our own minds, which is why it can feel so surprising to stumble on a parent crying alone in their bedroom or giggling with one of their friends – or to spot one of our teachers in a tracksuit buying ice cream at the supermarket at the weekend. These discoveries suggest an ordinariness and a vulnerability that we hadn't envisaged.

It can take a long while before we fully throw off our fantasies of others. Even when we are older, we may continue to feel that our pleasures and interests, our obsessions and worries, our love of silly stories, our enthusiasm for takeaway meals and our shyness or anxiety don't have equivalents in other people. This may give rise to stiff and solemn behaviour:

without really meaning to, we find ourselves making polite conversation about a prize-winning novel that we hate or cooking elaborate meals with heavy sauces that we would never cook for ourselves.

Maturity involves imagining something very remarkable and holding on to it tightly despite a frequent lack of observable evidence: that other people are, where and when it counts, probably much the same as we are. They too frequently just want to relax, chat about sweet and tender things and have a reassuring time over a tasty, informal meal.

The mature person knows how to be warm and natural because they look beyond the outward, impressive dimensions of a stranger and understand that there's likely to be someone just like them – just as silly, wayward, appetitive and odd (in a good way) – lurking beneath the facade. This is what gives them the confidence to suggest that we skip the three-course dinner – and have some takeaway samosas and masala dosas instead.

15. This painting, completed in 1817 by Jean-Auguste-Dominique Ingres, depicts a famous moment in French history when King Henry IV of France (on the floor on the right) was set to receive the Spanish Ambassador (on the left) but apparently kept him waiting while he finished a game with his children. How do you respond?

Jean-Auguste-Dominique Ingres, *Henry IV Receiving the Spanish Ambassador*, 1817

a) That's no way to run a country! What an irresponsible man.

b) Sweet.

56   How Emotionally Mature Are You?

Growing up is – in a sense – all about putting away childish things. We're no longer meant to drink hot chocolate, have pillow fights, talk to our teddy bears and dance gormlessly around the living room to unfashionable tunes.

Nevertheless, an over-rigid adherence to adult codes of behaviour may become a problem of its own kind. We may end up feeling sterile and dull, constrained and misunderstood, trapped within a rigid persona that doesn't give room to our natural contours. There is no such thing as true adulthood without the possibility of an ongoing connection with some of the emotions and sensibilities of our young years. A proper adult isn't someone who is never vulnerable, never playful, never confused and never idealistic; it's someone whose tender sides have been allowed to survive alongside adequate reserves of realism and practicality.

Henry IV of France (1553–1610) is commonly remembered as one of France's greatest kings. He was also notoriously unstuffy and, in one celebrated incident, kept the Spanish Ambassador waiting while he finished a game with his children. He had not lost his mind. Instead, he was signalling (300 years before such ideas became common) that childhood is a state full of significant insights and perspectives that big people overlook at their peril and should nurture in themselves in order to remain balanced and multifaceted.

It can be only too easy to evolve into the sort of grown-up who shows too much enthusiasm for the outward signs of adulthood – and therefore never allows themselves the liberty to giggle, jump up and down or wonder open-mindedly about naive schemes to reform the world.

This reserve may come down to childhoods that were so filled with disappointment and difficulty that they bred a wish never to encounter vulnerability and openness again.

We do our complexity greater justice when we can dare to pay selective visits back to the past – and, in the safety of our families and friendships, risk times when we pretend to be a rabbit or a blackbird, a camel or a horse.

16. You're staying at a friend's house. On the shelf in the guest bedroom are copies of:

- Martin Heidegger's *Being and Time*
- Søren Kierkegaard's *Either/Or*
- Ludwig Wittgenstein's *Tractatus Logico-Philosophicus*
- a travel magazine

Which would you be more likely to flick through?

---

a) The philosophy books.

---

b) The travel magazine.

It is hard to imagine that there could be any such thing as excessive intelligence. After all, most of the problems of the world and of individual lives clearly come down to a shortfall in cleverness – and a surfeit of impulsiveness, self-righteousness and cruelty.

Yet it seems that there could still be a way of using our intelligence that cuts us off from necessary encounters with simple truths about us: with humdrum facts, with down-to-earth ideas and appetites, with unglamorous impulses and naive yet profound speculations. If we can put it another way, there might be ways of being intelligent that could – at points – render us distinctively stupid.

There is a kind of person who we can dub over-intellectual, whose very cleverness can encourage them to miss key points. It may make them blind to obvious ideas that are nevertheless significant. It may give them a permanent taste for what is abstruse and infinitely subtle – at the expense of anything that doesn't pass an exaggerated threshold of convolution. They may neglect the chance of an interesting conversation with a 6-year-old because their associations of intelligence are rigidly affixed to scholarliness – or they might disdain the offer of a walk with their aunt because she left school at 16 and has never taken an interest in politics. Their intricate minds may end up misunderstanding reality, which comprises both Ludwig Wittgenstein and hot baths, Immanuel Kant and *Dancing Queen*, Aristotle and orange and polenta cake.

The over-intellectual may spend hours parsing the distinction between free will and determinism; they may devote themselves to interpreting Maxwell's theory of electricity and magnetism – and yet still be a novice when it comes to explaining their heart or avoiding a sulk.

True cleverness means resorting to complexity when, but only when, it is called for – and otherwise keeping room open for ways of speaking and thinking that are appropriately basic and visceral. It may be highly fitting to use riddles and jargon when one is dealing with the operations of a nuclear reactor or the nature of time at the edges of the universe. But it becomes a particular form of obtuseness to remain in such a register when unpicking issues in relationships or family dynamics. The properly intelligent can accept that there are central truths about every life that can and should be expressed in the language of a child.

It is an achievement to sound very clever. It may be an even greater one to know where and when to remain heart-stirringly simple.

17.   Are human beings all idiots in the end?

---

a)   No, why would we be?

---

b)   Of course.

We could associate maturity with a high degree of self-respect. Why, after all, would we not try to think well of ourselves and look with appreciation at our powers of reasoning, foresight and goodness?

There may be something that is even more important than self-respect, however: honesty. With this quality as our guide, it becomes hard to remain entirely serious and reverential towards ourselves – or indeed any other member of our species. From close up, without masks or deception, we are all comedically flawed propositions. Reasons to identify ourselves as absurd abound. We are a laughable mixture of high ideals and low motives, big dreams and humdrum realities. Our heads are in the clouds, but we can be swiftly brought down to earth by a rumbling stomach or the sight of an alluring stranger. We want to change the world, understand the mysteries of time and space and rescue humanity, but we're also distracted by gossip, upset by any ruffling of our vanity and incurably lazy and petty. We make solemn vows that we break the moment a temptation comes into view. We fart regularly and have hairs that grow in strange places. We lose heart because we develop a spot on our chin. We can't forget an insult that someone levelled at us fifteen years before. We're alternately moved by trivialities and left cold by genuine tragedy. We can rarely resist another slice of cake.

What choice would any frank human have – on the basis of this and so much else – other than to declare themselves a committed fool?

It is touching that we might be offended by the idea; it suggests that we still sincerely think that we could be serious, resolute and dignified.

But as no such option seems to be on the cards, rather than refusing to laugh, we should strive to stay one step ahead of our absurdity by opening up about our comedic aspects at once and with amiable resignation and apology. We should not have to wait for life to call us out as blockheads – we should, with kindness and compassion, own up to our silliness long before anyone else might be tempted to identify it for us.

18. A member of your team at work is underperforming. You like them as a person. Nevertheless, their presence is a danger to the business. However, standing up to them is very hard. What do you do?

a) Perhaps the problem will improve in time.

b) Take them aside for a difficult conversation.

It's natural and beautiful to strive to be a nice person. In a world full of cruelty and thoughtlessness, nice people are committed to being generous, sympathetic and gentle. They never want to cause anyone to feel defeated or to lose sleep. They will go to great lengths to spare other people tears. It sounds especially lovely.

Nevertheless, it is impossible to go through the whole of life being nothing but kind. Sooner or later, we are all called upon to take decisions that, even as they protect things we very much care about, will ruffle feathers, generate upset and may lead us to be (at least for a time) violently hated in some quarters.

We might, for example, have to tell a romantic partner that, in spite of our deep affection for them, we don't see ourselves being together for the long term. Or we might have to tell a child that it is now bedtime and that there can be no more stories. Or we might have to explain to a colleague that we don't see them fitting into a team and that they might be better off looking for opportunities elsewhere.

Such situations can be agony for committedly 'nice' people. There are great temptations to delay the moment of truth or avoid it altogether. Nice people still hope, deep down, that they can – while always smiling and agreeing – stay friends with everyone. Their distinctive sensitivity will have often been fostered by childhoods in which the consequences of being honest and forthright were especially difficult. They might have had a parent who flew into a rage or threatened suicide whenever an awkward idea was laid before them – perfect preparation for an adulthood in which there appears to be no option but to tell everyone what they want to hear.

However, being truly nice involves something 'nicer' still than constant agreement and emollience. It means signalling to others what one's value system is and sticking by it, even at the occasional cost of public opposition. It means taking on the burden of telling others where we stand and ruining their afternoon or month in order to save their long-term future and our own. It means accepting that there might be choices to be made between loyalty and sincerity, between bonhomie and effectiveness.

Mature people have come to terms with the tragic need to acquire something even more important than popularity: a character.

19. How good are you at putting up your hands and saying, 'I'm wrong'?

---

a) It's agony, really.

---

b) Getting better.

It often feels deeply implausible that we might – over some very large and important things – have got matters substantially wrong. Our minds have an avid tendency to frame situations in a way that flatters our aspirations and interests. Without quite noticing, we immediately take our own perspective to be the wisest in the room. We aren't deliberately bigging ourselves up; we're just hardwired to be on our own side.

It can take half a lifetime before we start to notice this fierce bias towards ourselves and can inch towards correcting it. In an argument with our partner, for example, most of our energy will instinctively be consumed by the imperative to prove them wrong; we will carefully search for evidence of why they are mistaken and why our will should prevail. But, with time, we might begin to keep at least a tiny space open for the peculiar idea that we may have ended up getting an issue back to front. What if we had misunderstood something key? What if, God forbid, we were the ones to have messed up?

Truly clever people know that they can only be clever some of the time. Scepticism towards oneself lies at the heart of emotional intelligence. Accepting that we might be a fool is a bedrock of wisdom. Those who best know their minds know that they do not work very well on all occasions, for they are filled with blind spots and distortions; they impose conclusions where none are warranted; they refuse to look closely at the facts and lack the nuance, integrity and energy to investigate problems to their roots. We are navigating through the world with the help of a very unsteady organ.

In the circumstances, knowing how to laugh at our own mind isn't just one quality among others. It's a central indicator of a capacity for insight.

We may well hit upon an important truth or two at times; but our chances of having done so are never greater than when we have first made ample efforts to imagine that we might be astonishingly wrong.

20. You suffer a strange and sudden drop in mood: you come to the view that existence is fundamentally an error, that human beings are incorrigibly wicked and that your life is substantially hopeless. What might explain such a mood?

---

a) A good look at the facts.

---

b) Have I slept enough? How is my blood sugar?

It's natural to assume that deeply felt beliefs must have deeply rooted and rational origins. But maturity suggests something more troubling and, in a sense, comedic. Much of what we feel at any given time is not the outcome of careful, rational examination and intricately determined syllogistic thinking. It's the result of crucial, but apparently humdrum, details such as how much sleep we got the night before, how our blood glucose is doing, when we last had satisfying sex, how our digestion is working and what the weather is like.

These topics can sound like insults to our higher faculties, which is why so-called clever people have historically ignored them entirely. Very seldom, at least in the history of the West, have our most intelligent thinkers counselled us – as wise parents will – to ensure that we get an early night, plenty of fresh air and a light diet composed largely of vegetables and fruit. We still await the Western intellectual who speaks in favour of a walk after lunch and speaks up in favour of sunbathing …

The emotionally intelligent, for their part, see no insult in being tethered to a body that has its own distinctive demands and which holds enormous sway over the motions of the mind. They understand that our entire philosophy will be altered by whether we get five or eight hours of sleep. They appreciate the possible mental effects of eating figs rather than hamburgers, and olives rather than crisps. They fully accept the role played by our sinuses and our bowels. They will always be as careful about what they eat and drink as they are about what they read and discuss. They allow a critical role for long baths in mental balance. They know that fresh linen and the smells of jasmine and lavender have their own contributions to make to a buoyant spirit.

A good life requires us to attend to some very large issues to do with politics, our careers, our reputations and our finances. But it must also allow space for what too often get dismissed as 'little things'.

The parents of young children know all about these little things – and that is why they appreciate that there is no point trying to reason with a child who is hungry or tired, and that the most urgent thing to do when wailing starts or crankiness grows overpowering is to draw the curtains and put on some soothing music – or hurry to the kitchen to prepare some stewed apple or mashed banana.

We should be as canny in managing ourselves. In moods when we feel convinced that our lives are over, we should – before taking drastic action – be sure to first explore whether we might badly need a twenty-minute sleep or a glass of orange juice. 'Little things' are – it turns out, and as the mature among us know – a pretty big deal of their own.

21. What might be the best way to become a more interesting person?

---

a) Read more newspapers, travel more and meet some high achievers.

---

b) Pay greater attention to your true feelings and thoughts.

Many of us crave to be more interesting people. The question is how we might become so.

We tend to associate being 'interesting' with achieving difference from the norm: with being able to serve up some unusual and intriguing stories and ideas. But what might be the best way to lay our hands on these?

One prestigious thesis tells us that we should try our best to root out new and well-reviewed books and articles, travel to remote places and befriend people who are prominent in the arts and business.

This correctly latches on to something – that we should aim to be different – but it entirely overlooks that, before we've ever read a single book, gone to any foreign country or met any Nobel Prize laureates, we are all compellingly different anyway. The problem is that we just don't allow ourselves to come across as such.

To get a taste for this pre-existing level of originality, imagine if we placed a microphone inside any of our minds and listened closely to the chatter. We would quickly find the most surprising and authentically gripping information: we'd realise that we are attracted to some very unexpected people, often just the sort we aren't supposed to have any feelings for. We'd understand that we have some hilariously personal (and shocking) takes on politics and society – and that we don't agree with most of the standard lines proposed to us by the media. Our anxieties, fears, hopes and excitements would reveal their properly distinctive and captivating pattern.

We are – though we try so hard never to admit this to ourselves, let alone anyone else – already a real character.

We understand this point in relation to children. Every child under 7 is fascinating. They almost never do anything interesting in the outside world, but it's the honest, uncensored way in which they report on their inner lives that guarantees their interest. When they chit-chat about their granny or their teacher or their take on their dad, we're open-mouthed.

We were once fascinating, too, before we became overly worried about seeming normal. As we grow up, there are, of course, some things that we should take care not to mention in order to spare others hurt, but a lot fewer than we think. When we next fear coming across as dull, we need only lean in more closely on the data from our deep selves: we should (and the habit may require a little conscious effort to develop) get in touch with what we actually believe. What emerges may sound odd, but it is also liable to be hugely charming, warm-hearted and comforting – and a lot closer to what people around the table deep down feel too than what was printed in today's newspaper.

Everyone is interesting. So-called interesting people are simply those who've allowed themselves to listen in on and share with others a selection of what is really going through their minds. They have not allowed self-hatred and self-suspicion to block them from disclosing their reality. They have been confident enough to imagine that the truth about themselves could be a pleasure for others to hear – and, with a few obvious caveats, it almost certainly will be.

22. A friend has recommended that you read a recent prize-winning novel. It's 700 pages long and about a very worthy subject. The book received many superlative reviews. Nevertheless, as one part of your mind recognises in the first twenty pages, it's very boring indeed. What do you do?

---

a) Plough on.

---

b) Drop it.

Almost without us noticing the pressure, we're constantly being encouraged to think extremely well of certain things: a restaurant in the centre of town that fuses Vietnamese and Peruvian cuisine, skiing holidays, a pair of trainers with specially cushioned soles, an unflinching novel about the American Civil War, a graffiti artist able to express his rage at capitalism.

It may feel incidental to locate a central theme of emotional life here, but a key determinant of maturity lies in our ability to relate sceptically to much of what we are told is worthwhile and good – and, accordingly, to hold on much more tightly than is usual to our own independent centres of enthusiasm and distaste.

Small children are masters of authenticity. They feel no compunction about taking a sip of a new drink and screaming 'Yuck!' or labelling a film 'boring' after only a few scenes. No doubt certain things of value get lost in the process, but something far more important is being exercised: a capacity to be, and to feel, real.

For too many of us, authenticity was early on sacrificed on an altar of propriety. Our parents may have given us strong signals that we needed to fall into line and parrot respectable ideas; our environment may have afforded us no opportunity to keep saying what we thought. We haven't merely suppressed our true feelings; we have lost sight of such feelings altogether.

When reading an insufferable novel by a prize-laden author, the last thing on our minds is whether or not we are being stimulated. We no longer treat ourselves as the central guides to what is valuable. We only recall the verdict of the newspaper's lead reviewer.

It's a sign of emotional maturity to have given up trying to be typical about pleasure – to be able to say that we hate parties or ballroom dances, beach holidays or museum visits, ballet or rap music – and not to care too much about the consequences. It is no doubt an achievement of a sort to have a wide cultural repertoire; it's an even greater achievement to understand, and to be able to admit without embarrassment, all the many self-important things that bore us deeply.

23. Do you lead a selfish life?

a) I try hard not to.

b) I want to give it more of a go.

The accepted story of selfishness tells us that we are – all of us – very guilty of the behaviour. We are apparently incurably addicted to our own satisfactions – and deserve to be compared unfavourably to pretty much any generation that ever walked the earth.

It sounds compelling (self-flagellation usually does), but the reality may be somewhat different. Whatever the risks of excessive self-absorption and inordinate pleasure-seeking, the real danger for most people is not that they too often ignore society and other people in the name of their own needs, but precisely the opposite: that they constantly put aside self-exploration and authentic inner development for the whims of so-called respectable opinion and socially sanctioned duties and commitments. The chief problem is not that we're too selfish, but that we're poor versions of what we might be because we're not selfish enough.

We spend our lives spending time with people we have nothing in common with, working at jobs that don't make sense to us, craving the approval of parental figures who have other priorities, going to parties we fear, sucking up to colleagues we hate, going to films that bore us, parroting opinions we're suspicious of, taking holidays that we don't enjoy and devoting ourselves to children who end up either indifferent or plain resentful about the care we've devoted to them.

Finally, in the last decade or so of life, we may try to 'live for ourselves', but by then, it's almost always too late.

Our connections to our own tastes and centres of pleasure and interest have atrophied, we've forgotten how to be ambitious in our own names, we've frittered ourselves away through millions of demands. We are alive, but we hardly exist any longer. We settle on golf.

Our priority, while time allows, should therefore be to acquire the skill of being politely but energetically more selfish. We should – from today – simply stop seeing people we dislike and stop worrying to such an extent about the opinions of strangers. We should focus on what feels meaningful to us. We should ask ourselves what we will wish we had done when we are on our deathbeds – and do it now. We should wonder what we would do next if we had blanket permission – and go ahead and do it anyway. We probably know the life we should be leading already; we have just been hoping – and should stop hoping – that someone or something would come down from the sky and give us a definitive seal of approval.

We should acquire the art of being difficult, of smiling less, of saying 'no' more often and of leaving the room when we want to. The world won't fall apart if we neglect some of our commitments; perhaps we can afford to forget someone's birthday or to let the house get in a mess, fail to prepare a meal or suggest that a grumpy relative make their own way back from the station.

We have grown quietly ill, or at least dull of spirit, through constant acts of self-sacrifice. We no longer have as many years ahead as we once did. We have been 'good' for an age. We have allowed our fear of boundless egoism to blind us to the importance of developing faith in ourselves. It may be time to take some baby steps towards intelligent selfishness.

24. You're at a party where you know no one. How do you feel about the prospect of talking to a stranger?

---

a) Appalling.

---

b) I could give it a go.

Some of the reason why social anxiety develops more of a hold on us than it might is that it is frequently – and misleadingly – put down to something we call 'shyness'. The problem with 'shyness' is that it can sound almost inevitable – a burden that we have been allotted by nature and that we would be incapable of ever evolving away from. It can seem as though we are shy in the same way that we are left-handed or blue-eyed.

In reality, shyness is more the result of a basic intellectual error than of anything rigidly fixed in us from the outset. At the root of the shy person's inhibition is a core mistaken belief that other people are not fundamentally the same as them: a belief that others don't share their excitements, anxieties, vulnerabilities and fears and therefore cannot be approached innocently or understood easily. The shy person believes that others are made out of stiffer, stronger, more elusive material than they are – which gives the shy person no option but to fear and dread them.

In holding on to such assumptions, shy people are the victims of excessive trust in appearances. From the outside, it can often look as though certain strangers are extremely unusual and perplexing. They can seem stern, impervious to doubt, coldly stylish or frighteningly in the know.

But the post-shy are not taken in by surface appearances. They are able to hold on to a fundamental truth that whatever the outward evidence, whatever the intimidating exterior, deep down, other people will invariably be much the same as they know they are. These swashbuckling paragons were once small children too; they too will often be afraid and beset by cares, they too will have known longing and sorrow, they too don't understand certain important ideas and feel under-read, they too have to sit on the toilet every day. What we're seeing isn't an actual stranger at all, just a version of ourselves.

This is what enables the post-shy to go up to new people at gatherings and advance casually into dialogue, rightly suspecting that they will soon enough hit on a common kernel of character, and that they are only dealing with another example of a fragile human who – beneath their fancy outfit or job title – craves love, dreads humiliation and is no stranger to confusion and loss. The person might be the CEO of a bank or an Olympic athlete, but one will soon enough be able to get beyond distracting externals and locate the real person lurking within.

Being able to talk to strangers at a party isn't one skill among others. It's a sign that we've grasped something fundamental about human nature: that we are (thankfully) far from unique.

25. You realise that a colleague on your team has done something wrong in the way they formatted a document. How do you respond?

---

a) Curse their incompetence and laziness.

---

b) Wonder if you have ever explained to them what you want.

One of the finest things about being a baby is that our minds can be read by others. Without us needing to say anything, people around us will have a guess at determining what we require – and, typically, they'll get it right. They'll correctly surmise that we are craving some milk or that the sun is shining in our eyes, that it's time for a snooze or that we want to jiggle the keys again.

This may be highly gratifying and important to us in infancy, but it can set up dangerous expectations for the rest of our lives. It can breed in us the sense that anyone – especially anyone who claims to care about us – should be able to determine our deepest aspirations and wishes without us needing to say very much. We can stay silent; they will mind-read.

This explains a widespread tendency to assume that others must know what we mean and want *without us having actually told them anything clearly*. We assume that our lover must know what we're upset about, that our friends should realise where our sensitivities lie and that our colleagues must intuitively grasp how we want things done in presentations.

Furthermore, we assume that if they don't, then it must be a sign that they are being wicked, deliberately obtuse or stupid – and we are therefore justified in falling into a sulk, that curious pattern of behaviour whereby we punish people for having committed offences whose precise nature we refuse to reveal to them.

Somewhere along the path of our development, we have forgotten the fundamental importance of teaching. Teaching isn't just a distinctive profession focused on imparting knowledge about science and the humanities to the under 18s. It's a skill that we must put into practice every day of our lives – and the subject we must laboriously and patiently become experts in and deliver 'lessons' on is called 'ourselves': what we like, what we're scared of, what we're hopeful about, what we want from the world and how we look for things to be formatted ...

Babies, for all their intelligence and charm, only care about a handful of things; an average adult has thousands of very set ideas on all manner of topics, from the right way to govern a country to the right way to shut the fridge door. We should strive to deliver a few 'seminars' on our views before allowing ourselves to grow resentful and sullen.

Yet how understandable it is that we should fail so badly in our teaching duties. We're not necessarily being lazy or unkind. It's merely unbelievable that strangers would actually require us to talk them through yet another chapter of the dense instruction manual of our deep selves. We never had to bother with all that in the early years. We may be more nostalgic for our infancy than we might have dared to imagine.

26. **When is the best time to bring up a complaint or issue with someone?**

---

a) The moment it occurs. We should get things off our chest.

---

b) The moment we don't mind any more.

The world is filled with people passionately disclosing matters of great importance at the very moment when these feel most urgent. At 1 a.m. in the kitchen of a suburban house, surrounded by the detritus of a dinner party, a spouse (who has drunk too much) will try to explain to their equally tipsy partner why they were severely offended by an anecdote about their mother-in-law over desert or can't take their sarcasm or taste in shoes any longer. In an office, right after a junior has handed in a sloppy piece of work, a supervisor will pull together an email detailing exactly how ungrateful and entitled this new employee is – and will rush to press 'send' before the day is done.

Our commitment to shouting late at night or hurrying to send brutal messages often has tender origins: it is the result of a fear of our own passivity. We so swiftly disclose our anger and frustration because we don't trust ourselves to hold on to a misdeed once time has passed and our temper has subsided. We set sail on intense currents of frustration because we are aware of an underlying tendency to forgive and forget too easily. We surrender to our rage because we suspect we are a push-over.

We lack experience of being at once calm and resolute, self-possessed and determined. We are either rabid or else resigned. Our indignation is a symptom of a lack of belief in our capacity for cautious, steady complaint.

Paradoxically, the optimal time for complaint is almost always when we don't care so much any more about what has riled us. So long as it seems that we cannot live another second around our maddening spouse or colleague, we should take immense care to fall silent. The essential ingredients of relaxed (and therefore effective) instruction are indifference and pessimism. It's when we can bear that we won't be heard and have accepted that most people – even quite well-meaning ones – will take an age to grasp anything, that we'll be ready to get things off our chest with the requisite composure. A month after a problem has emerged, when we almost can't remember the details, when the sun is high in the sky and our partner is at ease on the sofa, we should clear our throat and say, 'There was something I meant to bring up a while back ...'

People who shout loudly are, in the end, overly hopeful about the possibilities of interpersonal communication. To make a better go of our so-called lessons, we should strive to deliver them only in daylight hours, when everyone is sober, when we can break down our original sense of panic and bewilderment into a sequence of small, humorous and clear points – and when we have made our peace with the dark thought that we will always be substantially alone and misunderstood in a cold and indifferent universe.

27. Are you frequently envious of people?

a) Not really.

b) Of course.

A primary difficulty with envy is that no one sensible or kind is ever meant to have felt the emotion. 'They' – the awful ones, the ones who will end up in hell and who are inadequate and gnarled – of course experience it all the time, but we – the good and kind ones, the polite and hopeful ones – would never fall for such a noxious feeling. We're happy with our lot, we understand our advantages, we don't want for much; things are pretty good as they are.

And yet, considered more imaginatively, it would be pretty strange – and even distinctly blinkered – not to feel occasional pangs of intense envy in a world as diverse, rich and accomplished as our own. Never to look over our shoulder and want for anything whatsoever seems implausible when around us we can see exquisitely dressed people, boundless wealth and elegant houses – as well as people who are sending rockets to other planets, politicians who have transformed nations, entrepreneurs who turn out useful and lucrative gadgets and artists who can buy themselves private islands on the proceeds of their talents. To witness all this and stay wholly unperturbed smacks not just of admirable self-restraint but also of unrealistic and unhealthy denial.

True maturity relies on being able to admit and confront the full measure of our own inadequacy. Of course we lack a thousand things; of course we are frustrated and stymied in a range of areas. We must register our envy to be able to use it as a guide to our buried longings; envy alerts us to what we need to fight for. Everyone we envy is gifting us a piece of the puzzle to our as yet unrealised selves.

Even if we never manage to attain all that excites our envy (and we are unlikely ever to do so), accepting that we are radically incomplete prevents us from becoming internally bitter and deformed. So long as they aren't cleanly owned up to, regrets have a habit of releasing a sulphurous odour. We should turn our unrealised dreams into jokes (at our own expense), not angrily pretend that we are flawlessly happy with our modest lot and then acquire facial tics and a telltale tense and downturned smile. There is glory not only in achievement and renown but also in being able to confront our disappointment and sorrow without subterfuge.

Envying people isn't a sign that we're evil; it's evidence that we know ourselves well, that we can be honest, that we have avoided bitterness and that we have a higher than average chance of zeroing in on what actually matters to us. It's almost enviable in itself.

28. You read in the newspaper that a prominent person has made a slip in their personal or professional life (nothing too awful but not brilliant, either), and has as a result ruined their reputation forever. What do you instinctively think?

---

a) Serves them right. One less entitled jerk.

---

b) 'Let him who is without sin cast the first stone …'

There is a paradox to be confronted when thinking about who qualifies as a 'good person'. On the one hand, good people are those who respect the law, who are committed to tolerance and inclusivity, who have overcome their biases and who strive always to uphold the highest ethical standards.

However, there is a moment at which a commitment to being good can, in an unexpected way, become a problem in itself. There's a kind of devotion to goodness that is so zealous and ardent, so crusading and confident, so disconnected from modesty and a sense of fallibility that it tips over into blind self-righteousness. A good person can fall in love with being in the right to such an extent that they forget to be charitable to all that will inevitably be wrong inside every human heart – their own included. In their drive to clean out evil from society's stables, these so-called good people become rigidly offended by anything that is less than spotless. The list of unimpeachably pure and victimised people whom they feel deserve their kindness ends up being very narrow. They become monsters of an unexpected sort because they fail to acknowledge their own capacity for error and misdeed – and along with it, the imperative we are under to be good precisely to those who don't have an insuperable claim on sympathy or respect: those who might have been mean, angry, short-sighted and vicious but were still little babies once and now hunger for tenderness and forgiveness.

Really good people are kind not because they think that they are without faults and missteps but precisely because they have a rich idea of how bad they can be – and therefore marshal their memories when judging the wrongdoings of others. They know they are sinners, and on this basis are patient, tolerant, non-judgemental and sympathetic – in other words, properly good – towards a broad range of humans in difficulty.

It isn't a coincidence that self-righteousness is chiefly a problem in people under 35. Up to that age, especially if we are of a sentimental cast of mind, it is just possible to imagine that we are a lovely person. With good fortune, we can until then escape most of the heart-breaking compromises, ambiguities and desperate choices that belong to a complicated adult life. We may never have had to arbitrate between love and sex, money and success, meaning and acclaim; we might never have had to confront our vanity, lust or greed. Life can look very simple indeed, which is why we might have no hesitation in throwing large segments of humanity into vats of burning oil.

One of the key benefits of time is that we are forced out of this puerile moralism. Age shows us that we are all, in our own way, indubitable idiots, wretches and troublemakers. We end up being kind to anyone who is in difficulty because we know how easily we might have sinned – and might do so again in the future. At the sight of failure and disgrace, we put down our rock – and our hearts tighten with sympathy.

29. How much do you worry about the opinions of other people?

a) Quite a lot.

b) Not so much.

It is only natural to worry a lot about what people think: how they evaluate us, how they judge central questions of politics, what they admire and who they condemn. Yet much that is 'only natural' may have to be overcome before we have any right to qualify as civilised – let alone contented or liberated – adults.

Part of the reason why we respect other's opinions as much as we do is that we don't know them very well. It is rather hard to guess who is out there; we don't tend to know 'people' in general. We have direct experience of only a very small and edited group – our family, our friends, people we studied with or work alongside – and this limited circle may not represent humanity in its true dimensions. We might look down at a city from an aeroplane or glance out at a crowd on a busy shopping street and feel a general warmth and respect for the mysterious humans who surround us – and sweetly suspect that they must harbour fascinating reserves of wisdom, thoughtfulness and careful judgement. No wonder, then, that we might take their opinions pretty seriously when we hear about them via democratic verdicts, opinion polls, bestseller lists or 'likes' on social media.

But optimism about the sagacity and discernment of the human race rarely survives forensic examination. A detailed look at how people really think – especially as witnessed on digital platforms – will conclusively cure us of any illusions as to the quality of mind of the millions who silently frame our intellectual and moral horizons. 'Most people' appear to be strikingly furious, illogical, devoid of compassion and beyond reason. We may have begun with respect and humility, but if this is what the collective we know as humanity is actually like, we may well be advised to cut our own distinctive and emancipated path through the world.

Joy and liberation await us once we take the folly of our species properly on board, given how much we refuse to say or do, and how many desires we stifle, in the name of keeping on the right side of the majority.

We are not being snobbish in disdaining public opinion; we would happily listen, if we knew it could be sound. We may be ardent believers in the potential of every human to one day reason adequately – while insisting that most haven't learnt to do so yet. The reclusive 18th-century French philosopher Sébastien-Roch Nicolas Chamfort captured how great theoretical hope in our species might exist alongside fierce misanthropy: 'It is sometimes said of a man who lives alone that he does not like society. This is like saying of a man that he does not like going for walks because he is not fond of walking at night in the forêt de Bondy.'

30. You are promoted at work, publicly acclaimed or given extra responsibility. How do you feel?

---

a) Like an impostor.

---

b) Deserving.

Our sense of being an impostor is primarily fuelled by an imbalance in the way we face society: we know ourselves from the inside, but understand others only from the outside, according to what they choose to disclose or admit to us. This means that we are forever inclined to assume that, compared to anyone we know, we must be extremely strange, indeed close to freakish. We are aware of just how often we think of sex and of how peculiar our imaginings are as we walk down the street or listen to people at dinner. We have intimate knowledge of the deeply wayward ideas that flit across our consciousness: the plans we have for reforming the species, the extent of our despair, our bursts of naivety and optimism, our longings for love and the insistent beat of our many resentments and regrets.

But when we see others, we are presented with only the smoothest of surfaces. There might be an odd allusion to some 'difficult times' or a 'need for a break', but overall, the tone remains chipper and resolute. Vincent van Gogh put it beautifully in a letter to his brother: 'Does what goes on inside show on the outside? ... Someone has a great fire in his soul ... and passers-by see nothing but a little smoke at the top of the chimney.'

This disjuncture is at its most acute in the workplace. From our earliest days, we are liable to have felt frightened, foolish and always in a hurry to catch up on the basics – while others around us appeared serene, in the know and competent. Now, by a mysterious process that we suspect may owe something to error, we have been promoted to the very position of those who once impressed and intimidated us. We are now the head of operations, the chief strategist, the COO or, god forbid, the managing director – and yet, inside, we may feel no different from how we did in our first week, even in our first few hours at kindergarten. We may be dutifully doing everything expected of us – giving speeches, greeting new hires, writing position papers – and yet we are never in any doubt that we are, in our essence, just 4 and a half years old and about to be unmasked as an unremitting blockhead.

We can begin to build up a measure of confidence not by telling ourselves that we are, after all, solid and logical humans, but by accepting that everyone we have ever met – our parents, our teachers, our bosses – were all along just as crazy, fragile, excitable, terrified and silly as we know ourselves to be. There are no truly sensible people anywhere on earth; there are only people who are better or worse at hiding.

At this point we should probably concede that without quite meaning to, and with no evil intent, we may have contributed to the impostor syndrome ourselves. We probably haven't told our friends as much about what it feels like to be us as we might. We have never really explained to others what goes on with our bowels or the swirls of anxiety that visit us on pressured occasions. While inwardly focused on our insanity, we have simultaneously been making others feel like they are crazy: we have been links in the collective lie that seeks to deny public acknowledgement of the truths of human nature.

To overcome our impostor syndrome, we should hold on to the idea that others must – despite their stony facades – feel substantially as we do, whatever the degree of smoke that comes out of the top of their chimneys. And in the meantime, we should seldom pass up an opportunity to speak with greater honesty and fellow feeling about the turmoils and terrors of being alive.

31. You have been out to the cinema with a group of friends. It's now 9.45 p.m. One of the group says, 'Why don't we go for a drink?' Everyone agrees. But it's difficult for you. You want to go to bed; you're quite far from home and you have a busy day ahead tomorrow. At the same time, you don't want to be left out or to cause offence; and you don't want them to talk about you in your absence. What do you say?

---

a) 'Oh OK, but not for too long!'

---

b) 'I'd so love to, thank you, but I can't. I have a big day tomorrow.'

Life constantly calls on us to do things that don't entirely fit in with our plans: our child wants one more bedtime story, a colleague wants us to deliver a presentation (they tell us we would be so brilliant at it), someone we went on a date with wants to see us again ('it was such fun!'), friends want just one more drink in a bar ...

For some, there is no issue. If they don't feel like it, they simply say a polite but firm 'no' and move on. But for others among us, this is where the agony begins. How can we possibly turn down our hopeful colleague? How can we disappoint a kind date? What option is there but to drop our wishes and bend to proposals we secretly resent or despise?

Why do we assent as we do? Why do we find it so hard to lay down boundaries? At heart, it comes down to fear, fear that unless we do what others want of us, we will be in danger. Unless we read the child the bedtime story, they won't love us any more; if we disappoint our colleague, they will get angry; if we turn down our date, they could start spreading rumours and cause a scandal; if we don't join our friends, they'll think us a loser and ostracise us. We say 'yes' because we are terrified of losing love and facing hatred.

Put another way, we are – in the background – very unsure about our value and right to exist. We should pause, step back from our responses and feel a little sorry for ourselves. Our behaviour indicates that things cannot have been easy for us, most probably starting from early childhood. We cannot have been induced to feel very good about ourselves.

No one gave us a strong sense that we could be valuable if we declined a proposal or that, if people were to be unreasonable with us, we could push back and assert ourselves calmly but effectively. Through the prism of small social interactions, we glimpse a vast hinterland of damage and fragility.

The route out of the impasse is self-compassion and a commitment to liberation. We should dare to believe that friends will love us even if we were to say the odd 'no' – and that if they don't, we should never have had them in our lives in the first place. Whatever the situation, we have little to lose by asserting ourselves. At the same time, we should trust that were people to go sour on us for not doing what they wanted, we would not need to buckle, as we might have done when we were little children. We are adults – we can defend ourselves, we can make sure we aren't trampled on and can quash nasty rumours in the rare eventuality that anyone spread them.

It may not take long to have one more drink with friends when we yearn for bed – but we should take our inauthenticity as a warning sign that we have work to do on ourselves in order to grow more sure of our own minds and be less scared of society. It may not seem like much of an achievement, but the evening when we can finally tell those we are with 'You know, thanks so much, but I need to head home now' will be when, at last, we have learnt to respect, trust and love ourselves as – had we been more blessed – we should have done from the start.

32. A friend tells you about a party that was 'ridiculously glamorous' that they attended in New York. You haven't left home in a long while. What do you feel?

---

a) Provincial and out of the loop.

---

b) Fine enough right where you are.

It is tempting to feel that there must – somewhere – be a centre, a nucleus of interest, beauty, excitement and truth. Sometimes, this gets located in a particular city: New York or Paris, Luanda or Seoul. Sometimes, it is identified with a select profession: venture capital or tech, digital currency trading or abstract painting. And sometimes, it becomes synonymous with an age group: with being under 35 or (more likely) 22.

Inside the blessed circle, things are fun: life moves at a heightened rhythm, one is insulated from banality and routine, the cocktails come in vibrant colours. There's more sex, laughter and opportunity. The belief in this circle has knock-on effects in the real world: it shows up in the most concrete terms in property prices, which might be thirty times as high in one location as in another. It's why we might want to have extensive plastic surgery or buy a ruinously costly exercise bike.

The longing to be in the middle of things sounds like a joyful aspiration, but it's ultimately driven on by something sadder: a lack of confidence in one's ability to be an attraction in oneself. This state of being is perhaps the outcome of parents who looked to see if there was anyone else more interesting in the room the moment we were born. We aren't so much excited by the glamour of others as terrified of our own suspected mediocrity.

We can overcome our longing to be at the centre of things when we realise not that there are no differences between people and activities, but that these differences can't be neatly and categorically identified by the media and tightly restricted to a given city or social group. There are better and worse people everywhere, better and worse jobs in every field, and their distribution will always defy easy summary. One of the most intelligent people one could ever hope to meet might have left school with no qualifications at 16. A hugely dynamic individual might have a seemingly boring day job. Some of the most attractive characters aren't interested in make-up or fancy clothes. There are some very boring people indeed in New York and Paris – and some very kind and sensitive ones in Lucerne or the remote village of Osmoloda in Ukraine. Interest and appeal are scattered promiscuously and without obvious patterns across the earth. There is no one place where it could all be at.

We should develop a faith that, without any of the outward instruments of glamour, our lives and those of the people we like have the right to qualify as worthwhile. There is in reality no party to which we have not been invited; we don't have to fly to another continent or change profession. Every one of us can be a centre of something valuable already. Life is not elsewhere.

33. On a business trip in a city where you know no one, you are faced with having to go out for dinner by yourself. What do you do?

---

a) Think about it, then skip dinner and watch TV in your hotel room out of embarrassment.

---

b) Take a seat in a pleasant restaurant and delight in your own company and the chance to people-watch.

People who don't like themselves very much are never far from suspecting that others have worked out how disgusting and fraudulent they are. The person in the bakery knows that they are pathetic and peculiar – and has to stifle their disdain as they wrap up the loaf of bread and explain that they don't have any more doughnuts left. The taxi driver can tell that they are ridiculous-looking, unhappy in love, unhealthy and probably short of money. The new colleague has already worked out that they aren't very talented and are living on borrowed time. More abstractly, strangers and the world are endemically ill-disposed and are biding their time before they eventually give them their due.

The problem – as ever – does not spring from any external verdict. It is hard work managing a bakery, and the manager certainly doesn't have the time to analyse the possible personality defects of the furtive, blushing customer who hesitates before placing their order. The taxi driver is chiefly focused on their fare. The world has better things to do than to hate us.

The reason why we feel it must do so is because, to an extent we are unlikely to be properly conscious of, we seriously loathe ourselves already. We are therefore constantly on the lookout on the outside for what we intensely believe to be true on the inside: that people are out to harm us, that they are pointing at us and laughing, that they consider us absurd. We may not think of ourselves as paranoid – we don't think we are being followed by a government agency or eavesdropped on by spies – but we are essentially paranoid in the sense that we imagine evil intent in those we come into contact with. The last thing we conceive of is that people might find us sweet and touching – and want to hug us to appease what they sense of our anxiety and self-suspicion.

It may feel beyond doubt that the patrons of the restaurant have all stopped eating to look at us and to think of how wretched we are. But they have not. They are self-absorbed, indifferent and probably a little weary. If anything, they might like us. We have a problem – but not remotely the one we think. There is nothing to fear in eating alone; there is just much to regret in how we came to assess ourselves with such unsparing harshness.

34. How many stars are there in the universe, how many species have become extinct since the beginning of planetary life – and how much longer will the Earth be around?

---

a) This feels irrelevant here.

---

b) c. 200 billion trillion stars in the universe; 99.9 per cent of all species are now extinct; the planet has 7.5 billion years to run.

There is nothing more forgivable than making a big deal of who we are and what we have to do in the coming hours and days. Maybe we've got a project to finish before Monday or the light switch has blown in the bathroom or we have to send back a T-shirt we ordered in the wrong size. We're also pretty preoccupied that someone we wrote an email to hasn't answered back, that there is a pimple developing on the left side of our chin and that an acquaintance wasn't as friendly to us as they might have been when we ran into them in the street last month.

At the same time, our lives are playing themselves out in a universe with a diameter of 93 billion light years; if we had the right sort of spaceship, we would have to travel 236,000,000,000,000,000 kilometres to the closest galaxy, Canis Major Dwarf (the next closest is Sagittarius Dwarf Elliptical Galaxy, 662,000,000,000,000,000 kilometres away). The Earth has been in existence for 4.5 billion years, life began near a thermal vent deep in an ocean some 3.7 billion years ago, the first bird flapped its wings around 150 million years ago – and our lineage split from our first ape-like ancestors in Africa around 5 to 7 million years ago.

So, we may well have a parking ticket to deal with, the patio door might be broken, we could have had an argument with our spouse last night and our hair is thinning, but – in the wider scheme – we are a mercifully small and evanescent figure in the totality of cosmic time and space. We have no option but to take ourselves extremely seriously (we have to blow our nose and catch the train), but we have also been graced with a capacity to recognise, in our calmer moments, how profoundly irrelevant and absurd we are – and it is through this awareness of our finitude and nullity that we can reach our own distinctive grandeur and serenity of spirit.

Maturity doesn't just involve developing our faculties and understanding our characters: it is also about learning how to forget ourselves.

35. You start a friendship with someone and want to deepen your bond with them after a few weeks apart. What might you tell them when you catch up?

---

a) Something cheerful that has happened to you lately.

---

b) Something sad and worrying that has happened to you lately.

It feels natural to tell people we like or want to be close to about the happy things in our lives. When we meet them, why not hurry to explain to them that we will soon get a raise, that our relationship has had some especially cosy moments or that we have been offered free tickets to a premiere by a successful acquaintance?

Except, of course, that to do so shows a radical misunderstanding of human psychology. None of us is ever in any need of yet more information about how deftly other people might be navigating existence; none of us longs for further reminders of the good fortune and intelligence of their fellow humans. The media already tell us so much about inventors and actors, astronauts and entrepreneurs. We are all far too internally troubled, far too aware of our stupidity, missteps, unhappiness and longing, not to be severely offended and rendered newly lonely by tales of vindication and triumph. We're not being mean; we're just very sad, beset by cares and intensely lonely.

Those who know how to be kind to their friends therefore never hold back from sharing news of their sorrows and reversals – and may even exaggerate them a little in the interests of warmth and reassurance. It is the height of generosity to disclose ways in which one has proved to be a loser and a deadbeat recently. We should not be in any doubt as to how kind we are being when we tell our friends that we are getting divorced, that our business has failed, that our children hate us or that our health is failing.

Their subterranean joy may make them sound unfriendly, even vicious, but it is a sign of something far more benevolent and vulnerable: they don't know how to cope, they are feeling isolated in their confusion and regret and they are sure they are alone in making a mess of their lives. They may feel too embarrassed to let on about their pain without prompting, but inside, they are aching to find an echo of their failures in the stories we might tell them.

If we're going to go to the trouble of making a new friend, we should avoid the evident rudeness and blatant coldness of ever telling them that things are going well for us.

36. Where does true happiness lie?

---

a) A fortune, romantic love, career success, children …

---

b) A hot bath, fresh bread, dark chocolate, figs, walnuts, gardening …

Prestigious voices in society constantly call on us to focus in on the major goals we might aim for: a good relationship, a stellar career, a broad circle of friends. Normality has been equated with ambition. We are, by extension, prompted to be deeply suspicious of anyone who might claim that the meaning of their life lies in hot baths, quiet walks with friends, early nights or, heaven forbid, baking biscuits.

Nevertheless, experience and the passage of years have a habit of mocking our grander dreams: there are untold ways in which we can end up not having a career that delivers both personal fulfilment and financial reward. Those members of the human race who have secured genuinely happy long-term relationships could comfortably fit on a very small island. Rare is the parent who does not – in the quiet chambers of their heart – harbour extensive regrets about their children's development. Attempting to be famous and well-liked by strangers has similar risks to exploring the inside of an alligator's mouth.

After we have been frustrated, ridiculed and let down, we might turn with relief and new-found gratitude towards some of the smaller pleasures of which all lives can offer examples. We might not have found love, but we have music, autumn walks and history books. Perhaps our name has been disgraced, but we can fall back on gardening, French lessons and Scrabble. A prestigious job is desirable, of course, but a loaf of fresh bread can – for those who have shed some of their idealism and pride – be a source of joy too.

It would be a folly not to set out with the very highest ambitions; but it would be an even greater folly, in the face of the disappointments that are inevitably set to come our way, to refuse to genuflect to reality and to disdain the satisfactions that can be present in a modest destiny: be they those of apricots or walnuts, daffodils or lavender soap, whispered confidences in the dark or the hand of a young person we love. 'Small pleasures' can only be dismissed as small by those who have not yet suffered.

37. A friend you were starting to really like lets you down unexpectedly. It's surprising; you had thought they were wonderful in so many ways. How do you respond?

---

a) Cut off the friendship.

---

b) Sigh and reflect, yet again, on the good and bad in everyone.

There are few more tempting behaviours than to try to divide the world into two neatly contrasting camps: those of the 'goodies' and those of the 'baddies'. Furthermore, while we're prepared to accept that a majority of the people we will ever meet are going to belong to the latter camp, we feel justified in hoping eventually to find one or two that seem firmly and definitively to adhere to the former.

Yet experience is likely to frustrate any such aspirations. It appears close to impossible to locate anyone on the planet who will be as committedly and relentlessly good as we might have expected. There will always be something maddeningly wrong with everyone: an issue with punctuality or tidiness, intellect or politics, manners or insight, self-obsession or pride.

Child psychologists tell us that one of the great hurdles for toddlers is to accept the bewildering thought that their parents aren't ever either totally good or totally bad. The temptation in the early years is simply to assume that a parent must be either wholeheartedly brilliant or – when there's a tantrum – indubitably awful. It is highly perturbing to have to conceive that someone could be at once kind and annoying, both sympathetic and absent-minded.

Maturity involves conceding that people don't just have their strengths and, by accident, a few weaknesses, too: their weaknesses are a necessary and inevitable consequence of their strengths. Their qualities are inseparable from their failings. A friend will be irritatingly pedantic precisely because they are, at other points, touchingly reliable. Someone will be fascinatingly creative and then, as a logical by-product of their enchanting spirit, depressingly chaotic too. Every good quality has its corresponding vice. There can be no upside without a symmetrical downside.

In the wake of yet another disappointment, we may want to cut every imperfect friend from our diaries. But that would give misplaced hope too much authority in our lives. Maturity requires us to keep rehearsing for ourselves why perfect people cannot exist.

38. Are you always afraid?

___

a) In a way, yes.

___

b) Not too much.

There are so many objective reasons why we might worry about the state of the world and about aspects of our lives that we can fail to notice a more unusual and pernicious phenomenon: that of worrying all the time, far more than we objectively need to, in a remorseless, debilitating way, with a siren sounding incessantly in our minds. We do so because we are, as psychotherapists put it, *traumatised*.

Somewhere in the past of traumatised people, long before they were able to make sense of events, they underwent a shock (of a single or multiple nature) so great that their minds locked into panic – and they have not been able to let down their guard ever since. Perhaps their father raged at them, or their mother mocked them, or they were neglected and made to feel invisible. And now, to an extent they may not fully have noticed, nothing ever feels safe and the future is always on the verge of delivering an unsurvivable blow.

The particular objects of worry will change from person to person (and over the course of a single life), but the fact of worry does not. One person will worry that they will be disgraced in a scandal, another will fret about the state of their skin, a third will be terrified of running out of money.

Critically, the objects of current worry are never those of the original trauma; they are superficially plausible proxies that only reveal their delusional nature on close examination. In the meantime, the true catalytic incident has been forgotten, while continuing to cast its oblique shadow across the whole of life. We worry that 'everyone' may hate us, but carefully don't think – indeed can't think – about a specific set of individuals who were directly mean to us at the start. We cannot really remember the atmosphere of humiliation and shame of the early years; we just can't stop apprehending rejection in our careers and friendships. The unremembered past ends up manifesting itself as a panic-ridden future.

The cure lies in being able to return – usually in the company of a patient and sympathetic therapist – to the original trauma in order to understand it, gain perspective over it and feel compassion for ourselves because of it. We stand to realise the extent to which we are worrying now because we have forgotten what we were terrified of *then*.

We will be able to silence our alarm about the future when we finally work out how our past has unbalanced us – more than we have ever (until now) been able to imagine.

39. How free are you to sit with your own thoughts and explore your own mind?

---

a) Not so much – I prefer to have something to distract me.

---

b) I can wander fairly freely through my mind.

A crucial measure of mental well-being lies in the extent of our ability to wander around the rooms of our minds without too much inhibition or dread.

For some of us, without quite knowing why, there is something deeply unsettling about having 'nothing to do' – which really means having the opportunity for a lot of mental exploration, of which we're profoundly apprehensive. We get fidgety the moment there is no one else to talk to, the pace at work drops or the evening ends. It isn't that we love our friends so much; we're just scared to be left alone with ourselves. The idea of our phone running out of battery or there being no Wi-Fi on a long flight is more alarming than we can admit.

Unfortunately, avoiding the processing and digestion of mental material is no route to peace. We are forced to keep running one step ahead of our unthought thoughts while the badly repressed material of our minds shows up in ever more debilitating symptoms: we're unable to sleep, our thigh muscles develop a peculiar throb, the remaining ideas we are able to have become desiccated and unoriginal. We exchange perception for neurosis.

We're not refusing to think out of laziness – we are simply very scared. Offstage lies an unmastered morass of feeling – of fear, desire, regret or self-loathing – that threatens to overwhelm our powers of reason. We might be scared that we have to end our relationship, or reconsider a career in which we are already heavily invested, or accept that we are in a rage with someone we should love or are guilty of a deed we are searingly ashamed of.

We must own up to our reluctance to think in order to put in place the supportive and gentle conditions needed to help us take our first modest steps towards heightened self-awareness. We could schedule a long train journey and use the ever-shifting landscape to loosen our fears of getting stuck on any single idea; we might buy a journal and settle in a café, where the buzz of patrons coming and going can lend us a background feeling of warmth and freedom.

Ultimately, we develop the will to think when we recognise that there is no option not to think. What we call 'not thinking' simply allows the mind to drive its worries inwards, where they cause greater damage than would the examined thoughts themselves. Our minds are, by their natural operations, truth-seeking machines. They need ideas to be heard and will be a lot easier to manage when we can allow challenging thoughts inside the moment they start to knock impatiently at the door of consciousness.

40. Might you ever be – in your own way – mentally ill?

a) What a suggestion!

b) Maybe.

One of the reasons why our minds are collectively not as healthy as they might be is down to our exaggerated response to the term 'mental illness'. The most fearsome associations are to be expected the moment the phrase rears its head: we picture 19th-century-style asylums, wailing in corridors, doomed lives and irrevocable suffering.

But, in truth, mental illness is as common as – and should not be any more frightening than – its physical counterpart. None of us can expect to get through life without a run of colds, flus and aches, and yet we know these are generally survivable – and the very same should be thought true in the mental realm. There are psychological equivalents to a runny nose or a creaky knee. We should take on board in a sanguine spirit that there will naturally be periods in our lives, some of them intense, of anxiety, depression, paranoia, self-hatred and projection. We won't always want to live. We won't always be mentally well. But these things are as much a part of the normal functioning of the mind as are good humour, optimism and insight. They are the rainy days that belong to a healthy inner meteorology.

So, we should not compound our mental problems by refusing to accept that they have any right to exist. In the same way that most of us would benefit from a personal trainer and regular visits to a gym, so we should try to develop good reflexes of the mind by frequently parsing our thoughts in the company of a psychotherapist or turning to clever books, a journal or long baths to help us unpack the anxieties and apprehensions of the day.

The truly sane and healthy among us aren't those who angrily push away the suggestion that they might be mad. They are those who have reached a sufficient stage of self-understanding and have sat long enough with their eccentricities and extremities to know that they can shrug their shoulders and good naturedly reply, 'Well of course I am!'

41. How far into the future do you look when thinking of a better life for yourself?

a) A few decades.

b) A day.

It is hugely understandable if most of us are in the habit of projecting our plans for happiness on a timescale measured in decades. We picture where we might be in ten or twenty years' time – and imagine, within such generous spans, overcoming all manner of problems that beset us now: we'll have a nicer house, a more harmonious relationship, a sunnier group of friends, a better job, clearer skin ... Consequently, today doesn't matter very much; we're living instead in some undefined, faraway point in the later 21st century.

The emotionally mature don't conclusively reject this way of thinking, but they heavily modulate it, nevertheless. They have experienced enough of their own fragilities, of their tendencies to self-sabotage and of the furies and whims of fate ever to rely too much on the long term. Of course, they hope that matters will turn out well, but their wishes are tentative and modest in the extreme. Looking ahead to the future makes them feel distinctly queasy; they are frightened by the immodesty and recklessness of it. They are never sure that we are headed anywhere trouble-free for long.

Instead, the emotionally mature are prone to toy with far more restricted and manageable horizons. They like to concentrate on the day at hand. Their goal is to make it through to bedtime without too much anguish or alarm. Anyone who has ever looked after a small child or a very elderly person will recognise the habit. The difficulties of every moment militate against any lofty thoughts of the long term. They concentrate instead on ensuring that no one falls off the swings, that there is enough milk, that there are raisins in their bag and that they have remembered Nounou. Ten years from now feels very far away indeed. It can count as a big success to find an interesting piece of moss growing on a wall or a satisfying puddle to drop stones into. It's an event that a brown Labrador comes to say hello, its tail wagging in excitement and its tongue fascinatingly wet and extended. A highlight of the day might be the drawing of an exuberant and kindly-looking tortoise. Likewise, in the company of a 91-year-old relative, the principal goal might be to go out for a small walk in the park in the morning while reflecting back on the way it was just after the war. Perhaps afterwards, there can be a board game. Lunch might be some broth and a bit of leftover carrot cake. And when dusk comes, it might be time for a favourite film or a radio programme. We're not trying to do anything momentous; day-to-day living is an achievement enough.

We would no doubt be sacrificing far too many chances if we only ever thought this way; but we are also taxing ourselves unnecessarily and aggravating our levels of envy, alarm and confusion if we never allow ourselves to reign in our ambitions for a while in the name of getting through the coming hours. We need to be experts in both modalities of time. There will be difficult periods, when we should simply stop torturing ourselves with dreams of enriching, flawless decades ahead and properly appreciate instead the beauty, drama, challenge and love on offer to us here before nightfall.

42. How often do you think of death?

a) As rarely as I can.

b) As often as I can.

It can seem morbid and depressive, of course: why turn our thoughts to mortal considerations when around us there is still so much to enjoy and celebrate?

The equation is not, in truth, so stark or so diametric. We are not trying to think of death in order to hurry ourselves to oblivion; we are doing so in order to get a proper measure of the wonder and infinite allure of being alive.

The idea of death is the guardian of all manner of precious things that we otherwise simply could not hold in mind. With death firmly in our thoughts, we will never be in any danger of failing to appreciate the jewels that every passing day throws our way. We will notice the beauty of the sunset, the sublimity of the moon at midnight, the succulence of the passion fruit and the interest of the new book of poems … We'll remember to say thank you to an absent god for the warm summer evening, the autumn figs and the first snowfall of winter. We will not be in any danger of living with our eyes closed. We will be like someone saying a final goodbye to their old home in a foreign country, gazing more intensely than they have ever done before at the Cyprus trees, the azure skies and the limestone houses.

We are a spoilt species. It is hard – or close to impossible – to love what we always have to hand. We are ingrates who notice only what we have just gained or are about to lose. We can't see what is permanently around. And through such pernicious habits, we strip life of most of its flavour.

We are not being gruesome in thinking well of those earlier religious sages who put a skull on their table, looked constantly at images of the crucifixion or recommended regular trips to cemeteries. They were not trying to depress us, they weren't attempting to sink our spirits – they were wisely attempting to evoke for us the preciousness and cosmic significance of every passing day.

We will never properly accede to an appreciation of life so long as we think of it as a currency without end. We begin to know how many reasons there might still be to smile, how little should rightly alarm us and how many things remain to be savoured the moment we fully take on board that we are, with every heartbeat, being carried ineluctably towards our pre-ordained and life-enhancing end.

III.

SCORES & CONCLUSIONS

Having answered forty-two questions, aside from a small moment of self-congratulation, it's time to do some counting and award ourselves a score, which will place us into one of three categories.

Every question allows for two answers. The first answer, a), is the problematic one: it indicates a response that may be unhelpful to maturity. The second answer, b), indicates maturity and an advanced capacity for self-knowledge and development.

- Every a) answer should be assigned a score of 1.
- Every b) answer should be assigned a score of 5.

Add up your scores to identify which category you are in.

(i)   **161–210: You are emotionally mature**

The paradox is that to be truly mature means acknowledging the extent to which, in some areas, everyone remains deeply and irrevocably immature. There is no such thing as a wholehearted and enduring adult – only someone who can, every now and then, master their impulses for long enough to look at reality through a relatively untarnished lens and respond to other people with generosity and kindness. Nevertheless, if we have ended up in this category, we can congratulate ourselves on an uncommonly elevated degree of insight, wisdom and courage. To get to this point, we have no doubt suffered a lot, but we have also gained a distinct perspective on our suffering. We have managed to drain away our egoism and have replaced it with empathy and insight. We are experts at self-reflection and analysis. We have learnt to look at other people with charity and to feel compassion for the difficulties in their (and our own) early lives. We are no longer frightened of our own minds nor overly attached to the idea of always being 'sane' or, indeed, 'good'. Not coincidentally, we probably have a very good sense of humour, which we deploy not to humiliate or score points but to reconcile ourselves to the gap between the scale of our aspirations and what life is able to provide. We might have celebrated our 18th birthday rather a long time ago now (perhaps decades back), but we can be sure that we have reached a milestone of true significance: we qualify as a full adult.

(ii) 81–160: You are intermittently mature

In this camp, we are mature enough to accept with grace that we have a fairly long road left until we reach emotional adulthood. We know well enough our propensity to panic, our difficulties with forgiveness, our reluctance to reflect and our uneasy hold on reserves of calm and poise. We can be very effective in the outer world; very few people will spot our difficulties, but undoubtedly those who have had to live close to us will be under no illusions. They will have spotted the irritability, the unreasonableness and the proclivity towards self-justification and sulking. But we are not wholly stubborn, either. In our serene moments, we can acknowledge the problems; we are interested in our development; we are far from insisting on our perfection. We can laugh at ourselves, as we must. We stand to benefit immensely from continued self-exploration – we might invest in a journal, in a course of psychotherapy or in long meditative periods during which we can master the origins of some of our less fruitful patterns of thinking and behaviour. There should be no shame in our position in the rankings. We have come so much further than most humans who have ever lived; we are interested in progression and are well on the way to adulthood.

(iii) 80 and below: A way to go until you are mature

If we are in this category, there should be no shame in realising that, whatever the date says on our passport, we have not yet reached maturity. Very few people ever will – and at least we are here, in a place of reflection and committed to growth. The immaturity that besets us is certainly a problem for others: it comes out in ways that will make their lives far harder than they might be. There are episodes of unfair blame, of undue annoyance and of painful denial. But it is ultimately a greater pity for ourselves. We have a potential that is waiting to be unlocked the moment we can bear to look with greater courage within. We are far funnier, wiser, kinder and more generous than we have as yet worked out how to be day to day. We are driving the car with the brakes still on. It is a tantalising, promise-laden situation. Our minds are inherently geared towards growth; we are like plants with a destiny to push through the soil and up towards ever greater light. We should let them do what they already want to do. With emotional curiosity, we can evolve into the complete adults that we already appear to be to those who don't know us well. We can dare to evolve.

We might propose that in all our considerations of emotional maturity, there are twenty essential components. These amount to a checklist of key requirements for the wisdom and inner serenity we seek. We are mature when …

1.   We realise that most of the bad behaviour of other people really comes down to fear and anxiety – rather than, as it is generally easier to presume, nastiness or idiocy. We loosen our hold on self-righteousness and stop thinking of the world as populated by either monsters or fools. It makes things less black and white at first, but, in time, a great deal more interesting.

2.   We learn that what is in our head can't automatically be understood by other people. We realise that, unfortunately, we will have to articulate our intentions and feelings using words – and can't blame others for not getting what we mean until we've spoken calmly and clearly.

3.   We learn that – remarkably – we do sometimes get things wrong. With huge courage, we take our first faltering steps towards (once in a while) apologising.

4.   We learn to be confident, not by realising that we're great but by learning that everyone else is just as stupid, scared and lost as we are. We're all making it up as we go along, and that's fine.

5.   We forgive our parents because we realise that they didn't put us on this earth in order to insult us. They were just painfully out of their depth and struggling with demons of their own. Anger can turn, at times, to pity and compassion.

6.   We understand the enormous influence of so-called small things on our mood: bedtimes, blood sugar and alcohol levels, degrees of background stress, etc. And as a result, we learn never to bring up an important, contentious issue with a loved one until everyone is well rested, no one is drunk, we've had some food, nothing else is alarming us and we are not rushing to catch a train.

7.   We give up sulking. If someone hurts us, we don't store up the hatred and then hurt for days. We remember we'll be dead soon. We don't expect others to know what's wrong. We tell them straight and if they get it, we forgive them. And if they don't, we forgive them too – just in a different way.

8.   We cease to believe in perfection in pretty much any area. There aren't any perfect people, perfect jobs or perfect lives. Instead, we pivot towards an appreciation of what is (to use the psychoanalyst Donald Winnicott's exemplary phrase) 'good enough'. We realise that many things in our lives are at once quite frustrating and yet, in many ways, still eminently good enough.

9.   We learn the virtues of being a little more pessimistic about how things will turn out – and, as a result, emerge calmer, more patient and more forgiving. We lose some of our idealism and become less impatient, rigid and angry.

10.   We learn to see that everyone's weaknesses of character are linked to counter-balancing strengths. Rather than isolating their weaknesses, we look at the whole picture: yes, someone is rather pedantic, but they're also beautifully precise and a rock at times of turmoil. Yes, someone is a bit messy, but at the same time brilliantly creative and visionary. We realise that perfect people don't exist.

11.   We fall in love a bit less easily. When we were less mature, we could develop a crush in an instant. Now, we're poignantly aware that everyone, however externally charming or accomplished, would be a bit of a pain from close up. We develop greater loyalty to what we already have.

12.   We come to recognise that we are quite a difficult person to live with. We shed some of our earlier sentimentality towards ourselves. We enter friendships and relationships by offering others kindly warnings of how and when we might prove a challenge.

13.   We learn to forgive ourselves for our errors and foolishness. We regret the unfruitful self-absorption involved

in simply flogging ourselves for past misdeeds. We become more of a friend to ourselves. Of course we're an idiot – but still a loveable one, as we all are.

14. We learn that maturity involves making peace with the stubbornly childlike bits of us that will always remain. We cease trying to be a grown-up at every occasion. We accept that we all have our regressive moments – and when the inner 2-year-old self rears its head, we greet them generously and give them the attention they need.

15. We cease to put too much hope in grand plans for the kind of happiness we expect can last for years. We celebrate the little things that go well. We realise that satisfaction comes in increments of minutes. We're delighted if one day passes by without too much bother. We take a greater interest in flowers and in the evening sky. We develop a taste for small pleasures.

16. What people in general think of us ceases to be such a concern. We realise that the minds of others are muddled places and we don't try so hard to polish our image in everyone else's eyes. What counts is that we and one or two others are OK with us. We give up on fame and start to rely on love.

17. We get better at hearing feedback. Rather than assuming that anyone who criticises us is either trying to humiliate

us or is making a mistake, we accept that maybe it would be an idea to take a few things on board. We start to see that we can listen to criticism and survive it – and perhaps even occasionally learn from it.

18. We realise the extent to which we tend to live, day by day, in too great a proximity to certain of our problems and issues. We remember that we need to get perspective on things that pain us. We take more walks in nature, we might get a pet (they don't fret like we do) and we appreciate the distant galaxies above us in the night sky.

19. We recognise how our distinctive pasts colour our response to events – and learn to compensate for the distortions that result. We accept that, because of how our childhood went, we may have a predisposition to exaggerate in certain areas. We become suspicious of our own first impulses around particular topics. We start – sometimes – to distrust our feelings.

20. When we start a friendship, we realise that other people don't principally want to know our good news so much as gain an insight into what troubles and worries us, so that they can, in turn, feel less lonely with the pains of their own hearts. We become a better friend because we see that friendship is about shared vulnerability.

Also available from The School of Life:

How Ready Are You For Love?

A path to more fulfilling and joyful relationships

**A guided questionnaire to help understand ourselves
and our romantic relationships more clearly.**

Most questionnaires are just a bit of fun, but this one sets out to be both entertaining and useful. It offers us nothing less than a guide to the comforting and supportive relationships we long for.

Through a series of pertinent questions, it reveals our distinctive style of loving, what our strengths and weaknesses are with partners and how we might secure genuine fulfilment.

As we work through the questionnaire and its accompanying essays, we discover the many reasons why relationships go wrong, and how they might do so less often in the future.

Our minds are such confusing places, even the most thoughtful among us can fail to know central things about how we behave in relationships. This questionnaire will help us to understand ourselves more clearly and so set us free to discover the love we deserve.

ISBN: 978-1-915087-11-9

Who Am I?

Psychological exercises to develop self-understanding

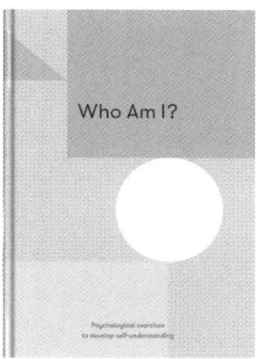

This journal is a tool for self-knowledge; a mirror with which we can study the most elusive and interesting parts of our complex inner selves.

One of the trickiest tasks we ever face is that of working out who we really are. If we're asked directly to describe ourselves, our minds tend to go blank. We can't just sum ourselves up. We need prompts and suggestions and more detailed enquiries that help tease out and organise our picture of ourselves.

This guided journal is designed to help us create a psychological portrait of ourselves with the use of some far more unusual, oblique, entertaining and playful prompts. The questions are designed to help us cumulatively appreciate how rich our identities are and how complicated, beautiful and sometimes painful our experiences have been.

ISBN: 978-1-912891-08-5

What They Forgot to Teach You at School

**A collection of the essential emotional lessons
we need in order to thrive.**

We probably went to school for what felt like a very long time. We probably took care with our homework. Along the way we surely learnt intriguing things about equations, the history of the Middle Ages and the tenses of foreign languages.

But why, despite all the lessons we sat through, were we never taught the really important things that dominate and trouble our lives: who to start a relationship with, how to trust people and how to cope with anxiety and shame?

The School of Life is an organisation dedicated to teaching a range of emotional lessons that we need in order to lead fulfilled and happy lives – and that schools routinely forget to teach us. This book is a collection of our most essential lessons, delivered with directness and humanity, covering topics from love to career, childhood trauma to loneliness. To read this book is to complete an education we began but still badly need to finish.

ISBN: 978-1-912891-39-9

Self-Knowledge

An examination of the importance of self-knowledge, providing practical exercises to aid self-discovery.

In Ancient Greece, when the philosopher Socrates was asked to sum up what all philosophical commandments could be reduced to, he replied: 'Know yourself'. Self-knowledge matters so much because it is only on the basis of an accurate sense of who we are that we can make reliable decisions – particularly around love and work.

This book takes us on a journey into our deepest, most elusive selves and arms us with a set of tools to understand our characters properly. We come away with a newly clarified sense of who we are, what we need to watch out for when making decisions, and what our priorities and potential might be.

ISBN: 978-0-9957535-0-1

To join The School of Life community and find out more, scan below:

The School of Life publishes a range of books on essential topics in psychological and emotional life, including relationships, parenting, friendship, careers and fulfilment. The aim is always to help us to understand ourselves better and thereby to grow calmer, less confused and more purposeful. Discover our full range of titles, including books for children, here:

www.theschooloflife.com/books

The School of Life also offers a comprehensive therapy service, which complements, and draws upon, our published works:

www.theschooloflife.com/therapy

THESCHOOLOFLIFE.COM